The Black Arts of the Gypsy

A Study

By

Various Authors

The Romani People

The Romani (also spelled Romany), or Roma, are an ethnicity of Indian origin, living mostly in Europe and the Americas. Romani are widely known among English-speaking people by the exonym 'Gypsies', as well as Ashkali and Balkan Egyptians (mainly in Albania), and Sinti (in broader central-Europe).

Although it is widely believed that Romani groups are of Indian origin, there are no chronicles of their early history, or oral accounts – and thus most hypotheses about the Romani's early migration history are based on linguistic theory and legends. According to one such legend reported in the Shahnameh (the national epic of Greater Iran) and repeated by several modern authors, the Sasanian king Bahrām V Gōr learned towards the end of his reign (421–39 CE), that the poor could not afford to enjoy music. He consequently asked the king of India to send him ten thousand luris; male and female lute playing experts.

When the luris arrived, Bahrām gave each one an ox and a donkey, and a donkey-load of wheat so that they could live on agriculture and play music gratuitously for the poor. But the luris ate the oxen and the wheat, and came back a year later with their cheeks hollowed with hunger. The king, angered with their having wasted what he had given them, ordered them to pack up their bags on their asses and go wandering around the world. The linguistic evidence has further indisputably shown that the roots of Romani language lie in India: the language has grammatical characteristics of Indian languages (especially Hindi and Punjabi) and shares with them a big part of the basic lexicon, for example, body parts and daily routines.

There have been many suggested migration routes from India to Europe, but it is thought that these occurred in waves, around 500 CE. It has also been suggested that emigration from India may have taken place in the context of the raids by Mahmud of Ghazni. As these soldiers were defeated, they moved west with their families into the Byzantine Empire. Though according to a 2012 genomic study, the Romani reached the Balkans as early as the twelfth century, the first historical records of the Romani reaching south-eastern Europe are from the fourteenth century. In 1322, an Irish Franciscan monk, Symon Semeonis encountered a migrant group, 'the descendants of Cain', outside the town of Heraklion, in Crete. Symon's account is probably the earliest surviving description by a Western chronicler of the Romani people in Europe.

In 1350, Ludolphus of Sudheim mentioned a similar people with a unique language whom he called Mandapolos, a word which some theorize derived from the Greek word mantes (meaning prophet or fortune teller). Around 1360, a fiefdom, called the 'Feudum Acinganorum' was established in Corfu, which mainly used Romani serfs and to which the Romani on the island were subservient. By 1424, they were recorded in Germany; and by the sixteenth century, Scotland and Sweden. Some Romani migrated from Persia through North Africa, reaching the Iberian Peninsula in the fifteenth century. The two currents met in France.

The early history of the Romani people shows a mixed reception. Although 1385 marks the first recorded transaction for a Romani slave in Wallachia, they were issued safe conduct by Holy Roman Emperor Sigismund in 1417. Romanies were expelled from the Meissen region of Germany in 1416, Lucerne in 1471, Milan in 1493, France in 1504, Catalonia in 1512, Sweden in 1525, England in 1530, and Denmark in 1536. In 1510, any Romani found in Switzerland were ordered to be put to death, with similar rules established in England in 1554, and Denmark in 1589, whereas Portugal began deportations of Romanies to its colonies in 1538. Later, a 1596 English statute gave Romanies special privileges that other wanderers lacked, and France passed a similar law in 1683. Catherine the Great of Russia declared the Romanies 'crown slaves' (a status superior to serfs), but also kept them out of certain parts of the capital.

Although some Romani could be kept as slaves in Wallachia and Moldavia until abolition in 1856, the majority were travelling as free nomads with their wagons, as alluded to in the spoked wheel symbol in the national flag. Elsewhere in Europe, they were subject to ethnic cleansing, abduction of their children, and forced labour. In England, Romani were sometimes expelled from small communities or hanged; in France, they were branded and their heads were shaved; in Moravia and Bohemia, the women were marked by their ears being severed. As a result, large groups of the Romani moved to the East, toward Poland, which was more tolerant, and Russia, where the Romani were treated more fairly as long as they paid the annual taxes.

During World War II, the Nazis and the Croatian Ustaša embarked on a systematic genocide of the Romani, a process known in Romani as the *Porajmos*. In 1935, the Nuremberg laws stripped the Romani people living in Nazi Germany of their citizenship, after which they were subjected to violence, imprisonment in concentration camps and later genocide in extermination camps. The policy was extended in areas occupied by the Nazis during the war, and it was also applied by their allies, notably the Independent State of Croatia, Romania and Hungary. Despite being 'Indo-Aryans', the Romanies were considered 'non-Aryans' by the Nazis. The total number of victims has been variously estimated at between 220,000 to 1,500,000.

Discrimination against the Romani people has continued to the present day, although efforts are being made to address them. Amnesty International reports continued instances of discrimination during the twentieth Century, particularly in Romania, Serbia, Slovakia, Hungary, Slovenia, and Kosovo. As a result, the European Union has instigated the national Roma integration strategy, encouraging member states to work towards greater Romani inclusion and upholding their rights.

Despite their substantial persecution and hardships, the Romanies have a rich culture, mixing Hindu, Christian and Islamic traditions, depending on the respective regions they had migrated through. Romanies are also heavily depicted in art and literature. Many fictional depictions of Romani people present romanticized narratives of their supposed mystical powers of fortune telling or their supposed irascible or passionate temper paired with an indomitable love of freedom. Particularly notable are classics like the story of *Carmen* by Prosper Mérimée and the opera based on it by Georges Bizet, Victor Hugo's *The Hunchback of Notre Dame*, and Miguel de Cervantes' *La Gitanilla*.

As is evident from even this briefest of introductions, the Romani people have a long and fascinating history. They have faced considerable adversity, yet have also left a strong cultural legacy and geographical spread. Their people and culture continue to expand and develop in the present day. It is hoped that the current reader enjoys this book.

BLACK ARTS

Black Arts

My Nurse's Song

OF fairies, witches, Gypsies
    My nourrice sang to me ;
Of Gypsies, witches, fairies
    I 'll sing again to thee.   *Scots Rhyme.*

The Art of the Romany

I 'VE seen you where you never were
    And where you never will be ;
And yet within that very place
    You can be seen by me.
For to tell what they do not know
    Is the art of the Romany.
                            Charles Godfrey Leland.

A Knowledge of Futurity

THERE was another pause, when the young Scot . . .
    asked Hayraddin, ' Whether it was not true that his
people, amid their ignorance, pretended to a knowledge of
futurity, which was not given to the sages, philosophers,
and divines, of more polished society ? '
    'We pretend to it,' said Hayraddin, 'and it is with justice.'
    ' How can it be, that so high a gift is bestowed on so
abject a race ? ' said Quentin.
    ' Can I tell you ? ' answered Hayraddin—' Yes, I may
indeed ; but it is when you shall explain to me why the
dog can trace the footsteps of a man, while man, the nobler
animal, hath not power to trace those of the dog. These
powers, which seem to you so wonderful, are instinctive
in our race. From the lines on the face and on the hand,
we can tell the future fate of those who consult us, even
as surely as you know from the blossom of the tree in
spring, what fruit it will bear in the harvest.'
                            Sir Walter Scott.

Noël

Sur l'Air des Bohemiens

N'AOUTREI sian très Boumian
Qué dounan la bonou fourtunou.
N'aoutrei sian très Boumian
Qu'arrapen pertout vounté sian :
Enfan eimablé et tant doux,
Boutou, boute aqui la croux,
Et chascun té dira
Tout cé qué t'arribara :
Coumençou, Janan, cependan
Dé li veiré la man.

Tu siés, à cé qué vieou,
Egaou à Dieou,
Et siés soun Fis tout adourablé :
Tu siés, à cé qué vieou
Egaou à Dieou,
Nascu per yeou din lou néan :
L'amour t'a fach enfan
Per tout lou genre human :
Unou Viergeou és ta mayré,
Siés na sensou gis dé payré ;
Aco sé vei din ta man.
L'amour t'a fach enfan, etc.

L'ia encare un gran sécret,
Qué Janan n'a pas vougu-diré ;
L'ia encare un gran sécret
Qué fara ben léou soun éfet :
Vèné, vèné, beou Messi,
Mettou, mettou, mette eici,
La pèçou blanquou, oussi
Per nous fayré réjoui :
Janan, parlara, beou Meina,
Boute aqui per dina.

The Three Magi : A Carol

To a Gypsy Air

WE are three Bohemians
  Who tell good fortune.
We are three Bohemians
Who rob wherever we may be :
Child, lovely and so sweet,
Place, place here, the cross,
And each of us will tell thee
Everything that will happen to thee :
Begin, Janan, however,
Give him the hand to see.

  Thou art, from what I see,
Equal to God.
And thou art his Son all-wonderful :
Thou art, from what I see,
Equal to God.
Born for me in the nothingness :
Love has made you a child
For all the human race :
A virgin is thy mother,
Thou art born without any Father ;
This I see in thy hand.
Love has made you a child, etc.

  There is still a great secret,
Which Janan has not wished to tell ;
There is still a great secret,
Which will soon be brought to pass :
Come, come, beauteous Messiah,
Place, place, place here,
The white piece of money
To make us rejoice :
Janan will tell, beauteous Babe ;
Give something here for dinner.

Soutou tant dé mouyen
L'ia quaouquaren
Per noSté ben dé fort siniStré ;
Soutou tant dé mouyen
L'ia quaouquaren,
Per noSté ben, dé rigouroux :
Sé l'y vés unou crous
Qu'és lou salut dé tous.
Et si té l'aouzé diré,
Lou sujet dé toun martyré
Es qué siés ben amouroux.
Sé l'y vés unou crous, etc.

L'ia encarou quaouquaren
Oou bout dé ta lignou vitalou :
L'ia encarou quaouquaren
Qué té voou diré Magassen :
Vèné, vèné, beou german,
Dounou, dounou eici ta man,
Et té dévinaran
Quaouquaren dé ben charman :
May vengué d'argen ou tan ben
Sensou, noun sé fay ren.

Tu siés Dieou et mourtaou,
Et coumou taou
Vieouras ben poou dessu la terrou ;
Tu siés Dieou et mourtaou,
Et coumou taou
Saras ben poou din noSte éta ;
May ta divinita
Es su l'éternita :
Siés l'Ooutour dé la vidou,
Toun essence és infinidou,
N'as ren qué sié limita.
May ta Divinita, etc.

Vos-ti pas qué diguen
Quaouquaren à sa santou Mayré ?
Vos-ti pas qué lé fen
Per lou men noSté coumplimen ?

Under these happenings
There is something
For our good, but of ill omen ;
Under these happenings
There is something
For our good, hard to bear :
One sees there a cross
That is the salvation of all.
And if I dare to tell it thee,
The cause of thy martyrdom
Is that thou art right loving.
One sees there a cross, etc.

There is still something
At the end of the line of life :
There is still something
Which Magassen will tell thee :
Come, come, gentle brother,
Give, give here thy hand,
And I will divine for thee
Something very charming :
But let the silver come, for
Without it we do nothing.

Thou art God and mortal,
And as such
Thou wilt live a very short time on earth :
Thou art God and mortal,
And as such
Thou wilt be a very short time in our estate :
But thy Divinity
Is for eternity :
Thou art the Author of life,
Thy essence is infinite,
Thou hast nothing that may be limited.
But thy Divinity, etc.

Wilt thou not that we tell
Something to thy holy mother ?
Wilt thou not that we pay to her
At the least our compliments ?

Bellou Damou, vèné eiça,
N'aoutrei couneissen déjà
Qué din ta bellou man
L'ia un myśtéri ben gran.
Tu qué siés pouli, digou li
Quaouquaren de joli.

Tu siés doou sang rouyaou,
Et toun houśtaou
Es dei pu haou d'aqueśté moundé :
Et toun houśtaou
Es dei pu haou, à cé qué vieou ;
Toun Seignour és toun Fieou,
Et soun Payré lou Dieou :
Qué podés-ti may eśtré ?
Siés la Fiou dé toun Meśtré
Et la Mayré dé toun Dieou.
Toun Seignour és toun Fieou, etc.

Et tu, bon Seigné-gran,
Qué siés oou cantoun dé la crupi,
Et tu, bon Seigné-gran,
Vos-ti pas qué véguen ta man ?
Digou, tu crésés bessay
Qué noun rousen alquel ay
Qu'és aqui deśtaca ?
Roubarian pu-léou lou ga :
Méte aqui dessu, beou Moussa,
N'aven pens-a bégu.

Yéou vèzé din ta man
Qué siés ben gran,
Qué siés ben sant, qué siés ben juśtè,
Yéou vèzé din ta man
Qué siés ben sant et ben ama :
Ah ! divin marida,
As toujour counserva
Unou sante abśtinençou,
Tu gardés la Providençou ;
N'en siés-ti pas ben garda ?
Ah! divin marida, etc.

Fair Lady, come hither,
We others already know
That within thy fair hand
There is a mystery very great.
Thou who art polite, tell her
Something pretty.

Thou art of royal blood,
And thy house
Is of the highest of this world :
And thy house
Is of the highest ; from what I see
The Lord is thy Son,
And his Father is thy God :
What couldest thou be more ?
Thou art the daughter of thy master
And the Mother of thy God.
The Lord is thy Son, etc.

And thou, good old man,
Who art at the corner of the manger,
And thou, good old man,
Wilt thou not that we see thy hand ?
Say, thou fearest perhaps
That we should steal that ass
Which is tied up there ?
We would rather steal the child :
Place something here, fair sir,
We have scarcely drunk to-day.

I see within thy hand
That thou art very great,
That thou art very holy, that thou art very just ;
I see within thy hand
That thou art very holy, and well beloved :
Ah ! divine husband,
Who hast always preserved
A holy abstinence,
Thou guardest Providence ;
Art thou not well guarded ?
Ah! divine husband, etc.

BLACK ARTS

N'aoutrei couneissen ben
Qué siés vengu dédin lou moundé ;
N'aoutrei couneissen ben
Qué tu siés vengu sense argen :
Bel enfan, n'en parlen plus,
Quan tu siés vengu tout nus,
Cregnies, à cé qué vian,
Lou rescontré dei Boumian ;
Qué crégniés, beou Fieou, tu siés Dieou ;
Escoutou, nosté a Dieou.

Si trop dé liberta
Nous a pourta
A dévina toun aventourou :
Si trop dé liberta
Nous a pourta
A té parla trop libramen,
Té prégan humblamen
Dé fayré egalamen
Nostou bonou fourtounou,
Et qué nous en donnés unou
Qué duré eternalamen,
Té prégan humblamen, etc.

XVII Cent. Noël.

A Gypsy Prophetess

NO sooner these remove, but full of Fear,
A Gypsie Jewess whispers in your Ear,
And begs an Alms : An High-Priest's Daughter she,
Vers'd in their *Talmud*, and Divinity,
And Prophesies beneath a shady Tree.
Her Goods, a Basket, and old Hay her Bed,
She strouls, and telling Fortunes gains her Bread :
Farthings, and some small Monies, are her Fees ;
Yet she interprets all your Dreams for these.
Foretels th' Estate, when the Rich Uncle dies,
And sees a Sweet-heart in the Sacrifice.

John Dryden.

We others know well
That thou art come into the world ;
We others know well
That thou art come without money :
Fair Child, let us speak no more of it,
Since thou art come quite naked,
Thou fearedst, from what we see,
Meeting with Bohemians ;
Why didst thou fear, fair Son ?—thou art God.
Listen to our farewell.

If too much liberty
Has led us
To divine thy fortune :
If too much liberty
Has led us
To speak to thee too freely,
We pray thee humbly
To give us likewise
A good fortune,
And that thou give us one
Which may last eternally.
We pray thee humbly, etc.

XVII Cent. Carol.

The Death of Richard Hunne

'WEL,' quod the Lordes, ' at the last, yet with muche
worke, we come to somwhat. But wherby thinke
you that he can tell? ' Nay, forsothe, my Lord,' quod he,
' it is a womanne; I woulde she were here with youre
Lordeshyppes nowe.' ' Well,' quod my Lorde, ' woman
or man all is one. She shal be hadde, wheresoever she be.'
' By my fayth, my Lordes,' quod he, ' and she were with
you, she would tell you wonders. For by God, I have
wyst her to tell manye mervaylous thynges ere nowe.'
' Why,' quod the Lordes, ' what have you hearde her
tell ? ' ' Forsothe, my Lordes,' quod he, ' if a thynge
hadde been stolen, she would have tolde who hadde it.

And therefore I thynke that she could as wel tel who
killed Hunne as who Stale an horse.'
'Surelye,' sayde the Lordes, 'so thynke all we too, I
trowe. But howe coulde she tel it—by the Devill?'
'Naye, by my trouth I trowe,' quod he, 'for I could
never see her use anye worse waye than lookinge in ones
hand.' Therewith the Lordes laughed and asked 'What
is she?' 'Forsothe, my Lordes,' quod he, 'an Egipcian,
and she was lodged here at Lambeth, but she is gone over
sea now. Howbeit I trowe she be not in her own countrey
yet, for they saye it is a great way hence, and she went over
litle more than a moneth agoe.'   *Sir Thomas More.*

The Gitána of Seville

YES, well may you exclaim ' Ave Maria purissima,' ye
dames and maidens of Seville, as she advances towards
you ; she is not of yourselves, she is not of your blood, she
or her fathers have walked to your clime from a diStance
of three thousand leagues. She has come from the far
EaSt, like the three enchanted kings to Cologne ; but unlike
them she and her race have come with hate and not with
love. She comes to flatter, and to deceive, and to rob, for
she is a lying prophetess, and a she-Thug ; she will greet
you with blessings which will make your hearts rejoice, but
your hearts' blood would freeze, could you hear the curses
which to herself she murmurs againSt you ; for she says
that in her children's veins flows the dark blood of the
' husbands,' whilSt in those of yours flows the pale tide of
the ' savages,' and therefore she would gladly set her foot
on all your corses firSt poisoned by her hands. For all her
love—and she can love—is for the Romas ; and all her
hate—and who can hate like her ?—is for the Busnees ; for
she says that the world would be a fair world were there
no Busnees, and if the Romaniks could heat their kettles
undiSturbed at the foot of the olive trees ; and therefore
she would kill them all if she could and if she dared. She
never seeks the houses of the Busnees but for the purpose
of prey ; for the wild animals of the sierra do not more
abhor the sight of man than she abhors the countenances
of the Busnees. She now comes to prey upon you and to

scoff at you. Will you believe her words ? Fools ! do
you think that the being before ye has any sympathy for
the like of you ?

She is of the middle stature, neither strongly nor slightly
built, and yet her every movement denotes agility and
vigour. As she stands erect before you, she appears like
a falcon about to soar, and you are almost tempted to be-
lieve that the power of volition is hers ; and were you to
stretch forth your hand to seize her, she would spring above
the house-tops like a bird. Her face is oval, and her
features are regular but somewhat hard and coarse, for she
was born amongst rocks in a thicket, and she has been
wind-beaten and sun-scorched for many a year, even like
her parents before her ; there is many a speck upon her
cheek, and perhaps a scar, but no dimples of love ; and her
brow is wrinkled over, though she is yet young. Her
complexion is more than dark, for it is almost that of a
Mulatto ; and her hair, which hangs in long locks on
either side of her face, is black as coal, and coarse as the tail
of a horse, from which it seems to have been gathered.

There is no female eye in Seville can support the glance
of hers—so fierce and penetrating, and yet so artful and sly,
is the expression of their dark orbs ; her mouth is fine and
almost delicate, and there is not a queen on the proudest
throne between Madrid and Moscow who might not, and
would not, envy the white and even rows of teeth which
adorn it, which seem not of pearl but of the purest ele-
phant's bone of Multan. She comes not alone ; a swarthy
two-year-old bantling clasps her neck with one arm, its
naked body half extant from the coarse blanket which,
drawn round her shoulders, is secured at her bosom by a
skewer. Though tender of age it looks wicked and sly,
like a veritable imp of Roma. Huge rings of false gold
dangle from wide slits in the lobes of her ears ; her nether
garments are rags, and her feet are cased in hempen sandals.
Such is the wandering Gitána, such is the witch-wife of
Multan, who has come to spae the fortune of the Sevillian
countess and her daughters.

' O may the blessing of Egypt light upon your head,
you high-born lady! (May an evil end overtake your body,
daughter of a Busnee harlot!) and may the same blessing

await the two fair roses of the Nile here flowering by your side! (May evil Moors seize them and carry them across the water!) O listen to the words of the poor woman who is come from a distant country; she is of a wise people, though it has pleased the God of the sky to punish them for their sins by sending them to wander through the world. They denied shelter to the Majari, whom you call the queen of heaven, and to the Son of God, when they flew to the land of Egypt before the wrath of the wicked king; it is said that they even refused them a draught of the sweet waters of the great river, when the blessed two were athirst. O you will say that it was a heavy crime; and truly so it was, and heavily has the Lord punished the Egyptians. He has sent us a-wandering, poor as you see, with scarcely a blanket to cover us. O blessed lady, (Accursed be thy dead as many as thou mayest have,) we have no money to purchase us bread; we have only our wisdom with which to support ourselves and our poor hungry babes; when God took away their silks from the Egyptians, and their gold from the Egyptians, he left them their wisdom as a resource that they might not starve. O who can read the stars like the Egyptians? and who can read the lines of the palm like the Egyptians? The poor woman read in the stars that there was a rich ventura for all of this goodly house, so she followed the bidding of the stars and came to declare it. O blessed lady, (I defile thy dead corse,) your husband is at Granada, fighting with king Ferdinand against the wild Corohai! (May an evil ball smite him and split his head!) Within three months he shall return with twenty captive Moors, round the neck of each a chain of gold. (God grant that when he enter the house a beam may fall upon him and crush him!) And within nine months after his return God shall bless you with a fair chabo, the pledge for which you have sighed so long! (Accursed be the salt placed in its mouth in the church when it is baptized!) Your palm, blessed lady, your palm, and the palms of all I see here, that I may tell you all the rich ventura which is hanging over this good house, (May evil lightning fall upon it and consume it!) but first let me sing you a song of Egypt, that the spirit of the Chowahanee may descend more plenteously upon the poor woman.'

Her demeanour now instantly undergoes a change. Hitherto she has been pouring forth a lying and wild harangue, without much flurry or agitation of manner. Her speech, it is true, has been rapid, but her voice has never been raised to a very high key ; but she now stamps on the ground ; and placing her hands on her hips, she moves quickly to the right and left, advancing and retreating in a sidelong direction. Her glances become more fierce and fiery, and her coarse hair stands erect on her head, stiff as the prickles of the hedgehog ; and now she commences clapping her hands, and uttering words of an unknown tongue, to a strange and uncouth tune. The tawny bantling seems inspired with the same fiend, and, foaming at the mouth, utters wild sounds in imitation of its dam. Still more rapid become the sidelong movements of the Gitána. Movements! she springs, she bounds, and at every bound she is a yard above the ground. She no longer bears the child in her bosom ; she plucks it from thence, and fiercely brandishes it aloft, till at last, with a yell, she tosses it high into the air like a ball, and then, with neck and head thrown back, receives it, as it falls, on her hands and breast, extracting a cry from the terrified beholders. Is it possible she can be singing ? Yes, in the wildest style of her people ; and here is a snatch of the song in the language of Roma, which she occasionally screams.

> ' On the top of a mountain I stand,
> With a crown of red gold in my hand,—
> Wild Moors come trooping o'er the lea,
> O how from their fury shall I flee, flee, flee ?
> O how from their fury shall I flee ? '

Such was the Gitána in the days of Ferdinand and Isabella, and much the same is she now in the days of Isabel and Christina.
George Borrow.

Meg Merrilies

SHE was full six feet high, wore a man's great-coat over the rest of her dress, had in her hand a goodly sloe-thorn cudgel, and in all points of equipment, except her petticoats, seemed rather masculine than feminine. Her dark elf-locks shot out like the snakes of the Gorgon, between an old-fashioned bonnet called a bongrace, heightening the singular effect of her strong and weather-beaten features, which they partly shadowed, while her eye had a wild roll, that indicated something like real or affected insanity.

'Aweel, Ellangowan,' she said, ' wad it no hae been a bonnie thing an the leddy had been brought to bed and me at the fair o' Drumshourloch, no kenning, nor dreaming a word about it ? Wha was to hae keepit awa the worrie-cows, I trow ?—ay, and the elves and gyre-carlings frae the bonny bairn, grace be wi' it ? Ay, or said Saint Colme's charm for its sake, the dear ? ' And without waiting an answer, she began to sing—

> ' Trefoil, vervain, John's-wort, dill,
> Hinders witches of their will ;
> Weel is them, that weel may
> Fast upon Saint Andrew's day.
>
> Saint Bride and her brat,
> Saint Colme and his cat,
> Saint Michael and his spear,
> Keep the house frae reif and wear.'

This charm she sang to a wild tune, in a high and shrill voice, and cutting three capers with such strength and agility as almost to touch the roof of the room, concluded, ' And now, Laird, will ye no order me a tass o' brandy ? '

Sir Walter Scott.

The Gipsy's Camp

HOW oft on Sundays, when I 'd time to tramp,
My rambles led me to a gipsy's camp,
Where the real effigy of midnight hags,
With tawny smoked flesh and tatter'd rags,
Uncouth-brimm'd hat, and weather-beaten cloak,
'Neath the wild shelter of a knotty oak,
Along the greensward uniformly pricks
Her pliant bending hazel's arching sticks ;
While round-topt bush, or briar-entangled hedge,
Where flag-leaves spring beneath, or ramping sedge,
Keep off the bothering bustle of the wind,
And give the best retreat she hopes to find.
How oft I 've bent me o'er her fire and smoke,
To hear her gibberish tale so quaintly spoke,

While the old Sybil forg'd her boding clack
Twin imps the meanwhile bawling at her back ;
Oft on my hand her magic coin 's been struck,
And hoping chink, she talk'd of morts of luck :
And still, as boyish hopes did first agree,
Mingled with fears to drop the fortune's fee,
I never fail'd to gain the honours sought,
And Squire and Lord were purchas'd with a groat.
But as man's unbelieving taste came round,
She furious stampt her shoeless foot aground,
Wip'd bye her soot-black hair with clenching fist,
While through her yellow teeth the spittle hist,
Swearing by all her lucky powers of fate,
Which like as footboys on her actions wait,
That fortune's scale should to my sorrow turn,
And I one day the rash neglect should mourn ;
That good to bad should change, and I should be
Lost to this world and all eternity ;
That poor as Job I should remain unblest ;—
 (Alas, for fourpence how my die is cast !)
Of not a hoarded farthing be possest,
 And when all 's done, be shov'd to hell at last !
John Clare.

The Sin of Gypsy Mary

NOW about Gypsy Mary, what I am going to tell you
is the real truth. One of the Prices she was, kinsfolk
of the Ingrams, and she married my Aunt Silvina's second
son, Black Billy. And she was a very poor fortune-teller,
and none of our people would show her the genuine way,
because she had such an evil tongue. So she had to do
the best she could to come over the gorgios in her own
way, and 'ticing them to do many a foolish little thing, to
get their money. And there was one time that she found
out a house to tell fortunes at, and she got a five-pound
note off the woman, and told her to go to the shop and buy
a pound of soap, and to go to some running water and
wash, and was to say, ' I wash myself away from God
Almighty, I wash myself away from God Almighty.' And
after she did that, the gorgie went mad, and she was taken

to the Denbigh Asylum, and died there. But poor Gypsy Mary had three years' illness for persuading the foolish woman to do such wickedness, and she was quite unable to walk during the whole of that time. When they used to be travelling, she used to be carried upon a donkey ; and her husband used to lift her up and down, and had a great deal of trouble with her. Still and all she used to chatter away like a magpie.

John Roberts, a Gypsy.

On Manner

A STROLLING Gipsy will offer to tell your fortune with a grace and an insinuation of address that would be admired in a court. *William Hazlitt.*

Hearing a Fortune

LIKE a queen the Gipsy woman sate,
　With head and face downbent
On the Lady's head and face intent :
For, coiled at her feet like a child at ease,
The Lady sate between her knees
And o'er them the Lady's clasped hands met,
And on those hands her chin was set,
And her upturned face met the face of the crone
Wherein the eyes had grown and grown
As if she could double and quadruple
At pleasure the play of either pupil.

　.　　.　　.　　.　　.

—I said, is it a blessing, is it banning,
Do they applaud you or burlesque you—
Those hands and fingers with no flesh on ?
When, just as I thought to spring in to the rescue,
At once I was stopped by the Lady's expression :
For it was life her eyes were drinking
From the crone's wide pair above unwinking,

　.　　.　　.　　.　　.

As still her cheeks burned and eyes glistened,
As she listened and she listened.

Robert Browning.

Mr. Pepys believes in Fortune-telling

Aug. 22nd, 1663. . . . After breakfast Mr. Castle and I walked to Greenwich, and in our way met some Gypsys, who would needs tell me my fortune, and I suffered one of them, who told me many things common as others do, but bade me beware of a John and a Thomas, for they did seek to do me hurt, and that somebody should be with me this day se'nnight to borrow money of me, but I should lend him none. She got ninepence of me. And so I left them.

Sept. 3rd. . . . And I to Deptford, and, after a word or two with Sir J. Minnes, walked to Redriffe and so home. In my way, it coming into my head, overtaking of a beggar or two on the way that looked like Gypsys, what the Gypsys 8 or 9 days ago had foretold, that somebody that day se'nnight should be with me to borrow money, but I should lend none ; and looking, when I came to my office, upon my journall, that my brother John had brought a letter that day from my brother Tom to borrow £20 more of me, which had vexed me so that I had sent the letter to my father into the country, to acquaint him of it, and how little he is beforehand that he is still forced to borrow. But it pleased me mightily to see how, contrary to my expectations, having so lately lent him £20, and belief that he had money by him to spare, and that after some days not thinking of it, I should look back and find what the Gypsy had told me to be so true.

Samuel Pepys.

Milton disparages the Art

IN his tenth Section he (Smectymnuus) will needs erect Figures, and tell Fortunes. . . . But he proceeds, and the Familiar belike informs him, that *a rich Widow, or a Lecture, or both, would content me* : whereby I perceive him to be more ignorant in his art of divining than any Gipsy. For this I cannot omit without ingratitude to that Providence above, who hath ever bred me up in plenty, although my Life hath not bin unexpensive in Learning, and voyaging about ; so long as it shall please him to lend

me what he hath hitherto thought good, which is enough
to serve me in all honest and liberal occasions, and some-
thing over besides, I were unthankful to that highest
Bounty, if I should make my self so poor as to solicit needily
any such kind of *rich hopes* as this Fortune-teller dreams of.
And that he may further learn how his Astrology is wide
all the houses of Heaven in spelling Marriages, I care not
if I tell him thus much profestly, though it be the losing
of my *rich hopes*, as he calls them, that I think with them
who, both in prudence and elegance of Spirit, would chuse
a Virgin of mean fortunes, honestly bred, before the
wealthiest Widow. The Fiend therefore, that told our
Chaldean the contrary was a lying Fiend.

John Milton.

Sir Roger's Line of Life

AS I was Yesterday riding out in the Fields with my
Friend Sir Roger, we saw at a little Distance from us
a Troop of Gypsies. Upon the first Discovery of them,
my Friend was in some Doubt whether he should not
exert the *Justice of the Peace* upon such a Band of lawless
Vagrants ; but not having his Clerk with him, who is a
necessary Counsellour on these Occasions, and fearing that
his Poultry might fare the worse for it, he let the Thought
drop : But at the same Time gave me a particular Account
of the Mischiefs they do in the Country, in stealing People's
Goods and spoiling their Servants. If a stray Piece of
Linen hangs upon an Hedge, says Sir Roger, they are sure
to have it ; if a Hog loses his Way in the Fields, it is ten
to one but he becomes their Prey ; our Geese cannot live
in Peace for them ; if a Man prosecutes them with Severity,
his Hen-roost is sure to pay for it : They generally straggle
into these Parts about this Time of the Year ; and set the
Heads of our Servant-Maids so agog for Husbands, that
we do not expect to have any Business done, as it should be,
whilst they are in the Country. I have an honest Dairy-
Maid who crosses their Hands with a piece of Silver every
Summer ; and never fails being promised the handsomest
young Fellow in the Parish for her Pains. Your Friend
the Butler has been Fool enough to be seduced by them ;

and though he is sure to lose a Knife, a Fork, or a Spoon every Time his Fortune is told him, generally shuts himself up in the Pantry with an old Gypsie for about half an Hour once in a Twelve-month. Sweet-hearts are the things they live upon, which they bestow very plentifully upon all those that apply themselves to them. You see now and then some handsome young Jades among them : The Sluts have often very white Teeth and Black Eyes.

Sir Roger observing that I listened with great Attention to his Account of a People who were so entirely new to me, told me, That if I would they should tell us our Fortunes. As I was very well pleased with the Knight's Proposal, we rid up and communicated our Hands to them. A *Cassandra* of the Crew, after having examined my Lines very diligently, told me, That I loved a pretty Maid in a Corner, that I was a good Woman's Man, with some other Particulars which I do not think proper to relate. My Friend Sir Roger alighted from his Horse, and exposing his Palm to two or three that stood by him, they crumpled it into all Shapes, and diligently scanned every Wrinkle that could be made in it ; when one of them who was older and more Sun-burnt than the rest, told him, That he had a Widow in his Line of Life : Upon which the Knight cryed, Go, go, you are an idle Baggage ; and at the same time smiled upon me. The Gypsie finding he was not displeased in his Heart, told him, after a further Enquiry into his Hand, that his True-love was constant, and that she should dream of him to Night. My old Friend cryed pish, and bid her go on. The Gypsie told him that he was a Batchelour, but would not be so long ; and that he was dearer to some Body than he thought : the Knight still repeated, She was an idle Baggage, and bid her go on. Ah Master, says the Gypsie, that roguish Leer of yours makes a pretty Woman's Heart ake ; you ha'n't that Simper about the Mouth for Nothing—The uncouth Gibberish with which all this was uttered, like the Darkness of an Oracle, made us the more attentive to it. To be short, the Knight left the Money with her that he had crossed her Hand with, and got up again on his Horse.

As we were riding away, Sir Roger told me, that he knew several sensible People who believed these Gypsies now

and then foretold very strange things ; and for Half an
Hour together appeared more jocund than ordinary. In
the Height of his good Humour, meeting a common
Beggar upon the Road who was no Conjuror, as he went
to relieve him he found his Pocket was pickt : That being
a Kind of Palmistry at which this Race of Vermin are very
dexterous.

Joseph Addison.

The Sibyl

DOWN by yon hazel copse, at evening, blaz'd
  The Gipsy's faggot.—There we stood and gaz'd;
Gaz'd on her sun-burnt face with silent awe,
Her tatter'd mantle, and her hood of straw ;
Her moving lips, her caldron brimming o'er ;
The drowsy brood that on her back she bore,
Imps, in the barn with mousing owlet bred,
From rifled roost at nightly revel fed ;
Whose dark eyes flash'd thro' locks of blackest shade,
When in the breeze the distant watch-dog bay'd :
And heroes fled the Sibyl's mutter'd call,
Whose elfin prowess scal'd the orchard wall.
As o'er my palm the silver piece she drew,
And trac'd the line of life with searching view,
How throbb'd my fluttering pulse with hopes and fears,
To learn the colour of my future years !

Samuel Rogers.

A Maid's Lament

LAST *Friday's* eve, when as the sun was set,
  I, near yon stile, three sallow gypsies met,
Upon my hand they cast a poring look,
Bid me beware, and thrice their heads they shook ;
They said that many crosses I must prove,
Some in my worldly gain, but most in love.
Next morn I miss'd three hens and our old cock,
And off the hedge two pinners and a smock.
I bore these losses with a Christian mind,
And no mishaps could feel, while thou wert kind.

But since, alas ! I grew my *Colin's* scorn,
I 've known no pleasure, night or noon, or morn.
Help me, ye gypsies, bring him home again,
And to a constant lass give back her swain.

John Gay.

Upon Cupid

LOVE like a gipsy lately came,
And did me much importune
To see my hand, that by the same
He might foretell my fortune.

He saw my palm, and then, said he,
I tell thee by this score here,
That thou within few months shalt be
The youthful Prince d'Amour here.

I smil'd, and bade him once more prove,
And by some cross-line show it,
That I could ne'er be prince of love,
Though here the princely poet.

Robert Herrick.

The Lady Purbeck's Fortune

HELP me, wonder here 's a book,
Where I would for ever look :
Never yet did gipsy trace
Smoother lines in hand or face :
Venus here doth Saturn move
That you should be Queen of Love ;
And the other stars consent ;
Only Cupid 's not content ;
For though you the theft disguise,
You have robb'd him of his eyes.
And to show his envy further,
Here he chargeth you with murther :
Says, although that at your sight
He must all his torches light ;
Though your either cheek discloses
Mingled baths of milk and roses ;

Though your lips be banks of blisses,
Where he plants, and gathers kisses ;
And yourself the reason why
Wisest men for love may die ;
You will turn all hearts to tinder,
And shall make the world one cinder.

Ben Jonson.

Narcissus

CEPHISUS. Speake then, I pray you, speake, for wee you
      portune
That you would tell our sunnfac't sonne his fortune.
LYRIOPE. Doe not shrink backe, Narcissus, come &
      stand,
Hold vpp & lett the blind man see thy hand.
TYRESIAS. Come, my young sonne, hold vp & catch
      audacitye ;
I see thy hand with the eyes of my capacitye.
Though I speake riddles, thinke not I am typsye,
For what I speake I learnde it of a gipsye,
And though I speake hard woords of curromanstike,
Doe not, I pray, suppose that I am franticke.
The table of thy hand is somewhat ragged,
Thy mensall line is too direct and cragged,
Thy line of life, my sonne, is too, too breife,
And crosseth Venus girdle heere in cheife,
And heere (O dolefull signe) is overthwarte
In Venus mount a little pricke or warte.
Besides heere, in the hillocke of great Jupiter,
Monnsieur la mors lyes lurking like a sheppbiter ;
What can I make out of this hard construction
But dolefull dumpes, decay, death, & destruction ?

Anon.

The Fortune-teller

A GYPSY I wuz born'd
   An' a Gypsy I 'll demain ;
A-tellin' young maids deir forchants,
   Myself I will maintain.

English Gypsy Song.

The Vicar's Daughters

BUT we could have borne all this, had not a fortune-telling gipsy come to raise us into perfect sublimity. The tawny sibyl no sooner appeared, than my girls came running to me for a shilling a-piece to cross her hand with silver. To say the truth, I was tired of being always wise, and could not help gratifying their request, because I loved to see them happy. I gave each of them a shilling ; though for the honour of the family it must be observed, that they never went without money themselves, as my wife always generously let them have a guinea each, to keep in their pockets, but with strict injunctions never to change it. After they had been closeted up with the fortune-teller for some time, I knew by their looks, upon their returning, that they had been promised something great.—' Well, my girls, how have you sped ? Tell me, Livy, has the fortune-teller given thee a pennyworth ? '—' I protest, Papa,' says the girl, ' I believe she deals with somebody that 's not right ; for she positively declared, that I am to be married to a 'Squire in less than a twelve-month ! '—' Well, now Sophy, my child,' said I, ' and what sort of a husband are you to have ? '—' Sir, replied she, ' I am to have a Lord soon after my sister has married the 'Squire.'—' How,' cried I, ' is that all you are to have for your two shillings ? Only a Lord and a 'Squire for two shillings ! You fools, I could have promised you a Prince and a Nabob for half the money.'   *Oliver Goldsmith.*

The Way of Soothsayers

PRIESTS and soothsayers go the round of rich men's doors and persuade them that they have power from the gods, whereby, if any sin has been committed by a man or his ancestors, they can heal it by charms and sacrifice performed to the accompaniment of feasting and pleasure, and if any man wishes to injure an enemy, at a small cost he may harm just and unjust indifferently ; for with their incantations and magic formulae they say they can persuade the gods to serve their will.   *Plato.*

King Bagrat and the Magicians

WHILST the pious king, Bagrat IV. [*c.* 1048], was in
the imperial city of Constantinople, he learnt—a
thing marvellous and quite incredible—that there were
certain descendants there of the Samaritan race of Simon
Magus, called Atsincan, wizards and famous rogues. Now
there were wild beasts that used to come and devour the
animals kept, for the monarch's chase, in the imperial park.
The great emperor Monomachus, learning of this, bade
summon the Atsincan, to destroy by their magic art the
beasts devouring his game. They, in obedience to the
imperial behest, killed a quantity of wild beasts. King
Bagrat heard of it, and summoning the Atsincan said :
' How have you killed these beasts ? ' ' Sire,' said they,
' our art teaches us to poison meat, which we put in a place
frequented by these beasts ; then climbing a tree, we
attract them by imitating the cry of the animals ; they
assemble, eat the meat, and drop down dead. Only
beasts born on Holy Saturday obey us not. Instead of
eating the poisoned meat, they say to us " Eat it your-
selves " ; then off they go unharmed.' The monarch,
wishing to see it with his own eyes, bade them summon
a beast of this sort, but they could find nothing but a dog
which they knew had not been born upon that day. The
monk, who was present with the King, was moved with
the same natural sentiment as we have spoken of above,
on the subject of the icons and of the divine representation.
He was moved, not with pity only, but with the fear of God,
and would have no such doings among Christians, above
all before the King, in a place where he was himself. He
made the sign of the cross on the poisoned meat, and the
animal had no sooner swallowed it than it brought it up,
and so did not drop dead. The dog having taken no harm,
the baffled wizards begged the King to have the monk,
Giorgi, taken into the inner apartments, and to order
another dog to be brought. The holy monk gone, they
brought another dog, and gave him the poisoned meat :
he fell dead instantly. At sight of this King Bagrat and
his lords rejoiced exceedingly, and told the marvel to the

pious emperor, Constantine Monomachus [1042-54], who shared their satisfaction and thanked God. As to King Bagrat, he said ' With this holy man near me, I fear neither wizards nor their deadly poisons.'   *Georgian XII Cent. MS.*

Mrs. Herne and the Grey-haired Brother

IT was about noon on the third day that I sat beneath the shade of the ash tree ; I was not at work, for the weather was particularly hot, and I felt but little inclination to make any exertion. Leaning my back against the tree, I was not long in falling into a slumber. I particularly remember that slumber of mine beneath the ash tree, for it was about the sweetest slumber that I ever enjoyed ; how long I continued in it I do not know ; I could almost have wished that it had lasted to the present time. All of a sudden it appeared to me that a voice cried in my ear, ' Danger ! danger ! danger ! ' Nothing seemingly could be more distinct than the words which I heard ; then an uneasy sensation came over me, which I strove to get rid of, and at last succeeded, for I awoke. The gypsy girl was standing just opposite to me, with her eyes fixed upon my countenance ; a singular kind of little dog stood beside her.

' Ha ! ' said I, ' was it you that cried danger ? What danger is there ? '

' Danger, brother, there is no danger ; what danger should there be ? I called to my little dog, but that was in the wood ; my little dog's name is not danger, but Stranger ; what danger should there be, brother ? '

' What, indeed, except in sleeping beneath a tree ; what is that you have got in your hand ? '

' Something for you,' said the girl, sitting down and proceeding to untie a white napkin ; ' a pretty manricli, so sweet, so nice ; when I went home to my people I told my grandbebee how kind you had been to the poor person's child, and when my grandbebee saw the kekaubi, she said : " Hir mi devlis, it won't do for the poor people to be ungrateful ; by my God, I will bake a cake for the young harko mescro." '

' But there are two cakes.'

' Yes, brother, two cakes, both for you ; my grandbebee meant them both for you—but liſt, brother, I will have one of them for bringing them. I know you will give me one, pretty brother, grey-haired brother—which shall I have, brother ? '

In the napkin were two round cakes, seemingly made of rich and coſtly compounds, and precisely similar in form, each weighing about half a pound.

' Which shall I have, brother ? ' said the gypsy girl.

' Whichever you please.'

' No, brother, no, the cakes are yours, not mine, it is for you to say.'

' Well, then, give me the one neareſt you, and take the other.'

' Yes, brother, yes,' said the girl ; and taking the cakes, she flung them into the air two or three times, catching them as they fell, and singing the while. ' Pretty brother, grey-haired brother—here, brother,' said she, ' here is your cake, this other is mine.'

' Are you sure,' said I, taking the cake, ' that this is the one I chose ? '

' Quite sure, brother ; but if you like you can have mine ; there 's no difference however—shall I eat ? '

' Yes, siſter, eat.'

' See, brother, I do ; now, brother, eat, pretty brother, grey-haired brother.'

' I am not hungry.'

' Not hungry ! well, what then—what has being hungry to do with the matter ? It is my grandbebee's cake which was sent because you were kind to the poor person's child ; eat, brother, eat, and we shall be like the children in the wood that the gorgios speak of.'

' The children in the wood had nothing to eat.'

' Yes, they had hips and haws ; we have better. Eat, brother.'

' See, siſter, I do,' and I ate a piece of the cake.

' Well, brother, how do you like it ? ' said the girl, look-ing fixedly at me.

' It is very rich and sweet, and yet there is something ſtrange about it ; I don't think I shall eat any more.'

' Fie, brother, fie, to find fault with the poor person's cake ; see, I have nearly eaten mine.'

'That's a pretty little dog.'

'Is it not, brother? that's my juggal, my little sister, as I call her.'

'Come here, Juggal,' said I to the animal.

'What do you want with my juggal?' said the girl.

'Only to give her a piece of cake,' said I, offering the dog a piece which I had just broken off.

'What do you mean?' said the girl, snatching the dog away; 'my grandbebee's cake is not for dogs.'

'Why, I just now saw you give the animal a piece of yours.'

'You lie, brother, you saw no such thing; but I see how it is, you wish to affront the poor person's child. I shall go to my house.'

'Keep still, and don't be angry; see, I have eaten the piece which I offered the dog. I meant no offence. It is a sweet cake after all.'

'Isn't it, brother? I am glad you like it. Offence! brother, no offence at all! I am so glad you like my grandbebee's cake, but she will be wanting me at home. Eat one piece more of grandbebee's cake and I will go.'

'I am not hungry, I will put the rest by.'

'One piece more before I go, handsome brother, grey-haired brother.'

'I will not eat any more, I have already eaten more than I wished, to oblige you; if you must go, good day to you.'

The girl rose upon her feet, looked hard at me, then at the remainder of the cake which I held in my hand, and then at me again, and then stood for a moment or two, as if in deep thought; presently an air of satisfaction came over her countenance, she smiled and said: 'Well, brother, well, do as you please; I merely wished you to eat because you have been so kind to the poor person's child. She loves you so, that she could have wished to have seen you eat it all; good-bye, brother, I dare say when I am gone you will eat some more of it, and if you don't I dare say you have eaten enough to—to—show your love for us. After all, it was a poor person's cake, a Rommany manricli, and all you gorgios are somewhat gorgious. Farewell, brother, pretty brother, grey-haired brother. Come, juggal.'

I remained under the ash tree seated on the grass for a

minute or two, and endeavoured to resume the occupation in which I had been engaged before I fell asleep, but I felt no inclination for labour. I then thought I would sleep again, and once more reclined against the tree, and slumbered for some little time, but my sleep was more agitated than before. Something appeared to bear heavy on my breast. I struggled in my sleep, fell on the grass, and awoke ; my temples were throbbing, there was a burning in my eyes, and my mouth felt parched ; the oppression about the chest which I had felt in my sleep still continued. 'I must shake off these feelings,' said I, 'and get upon my legs.' I walked rapidly up and down upon the green sward ; at length, feeling my thirst increase, I directed my steps down the narrow path to the spring which ran amidst the bushes ; arriving there, I knelt down and drank of the water, but on lifting up my head I felt thirstier than before ; again I drank, but with the like result ; I was about to drink for the third time, when I felt a dreadful qualm which instantly robbed me of nearly all my strength. What can be the matter with me, thought I ; but I suppose I have made myself ill by drinking cold water. I got up and made the best of my way back to my tent ; before I reached it the qualm had seized me again, and I was deadly sick. I flung myself on my pallet ; qualm succeeded qualm, but in the intervals my mouth was dry and burning, and I felt a frantic desire to drink, but no water was at hand, and to reach the spring once more was impossible ; the qualms continued, deadly pains shot through my whole frame ; I could bear my agonies no longer, and I fell into a trance or swoon. How long I continued therein I know not ; on recovering, however, I felt somewhat better, and attempted to lift my head off my couch ; the next moment, however, the qualms and pains returned, if possible, with greater violence than before. I am dying, thought I, like a dog, without any help ; and then methought I heard a sound at a distance like people singing, and then once more I relapsed into my swoon.

I revived just as a heavy blow sounded upon the canvas of the tent. I started, but my condition did not permit me to rise ; again the same kind of blow sounded upon the canvas ; I thought for a moment of crying out and request-

ing assistance, but an inexplicable something chained my
tongue, and now I heard a whisper on the outside of the
tent. ' He does not move, bebee,' said a voice which I
knew. ' I should not wonder if it has done for him
already ; however, strike again with your ran ' ; and then
there was another blow, after which another voice cried
aloud in a strange tone : ' Is the gentleman of the house
asleep, or is he taking his dinner ? ' I remained quite
silent and motionless, and in another moment the voice
continued : ' What, no answer ? what can the gentleman
of the house be about that he makes no answer ? Perhaps
the gentleman of the house may be darning his stockings ? '
Thereupon a face peered into the door of the tent, at the
farther extremity of which I was stretched. It was that
of a woman, but owing to the posture in which she stood,
with her back to the light, and partly owing to a large straw
bonnet, I could distinguish but very little of the features of
her countenance. I had, however, recognised her voice ;
it was that of my old acquaintance, Mrs. Herne. ' Ho,
ho, sir ! ' said she, ' here you are. Come here, Leonora,'
said she to the gypsy girl, who pressed in at the other side
of the door ; ' here is the gentleman, not asleep, but only
stretched out after dinner. Sit down on your ham, child,
at the door ; I shall do the same. There—you have seen
me before, sir, have you not ? '

' The gentleman makes no answer, bebee ; perhaps he
does not know you.'

' I have known him of old, Leonora,' said Mrs. Herne ;
' and, to tell you the truth, though I spoke to him just now,
I expected no answer.'

' It 's a way he has, bebee, I suppose ? '

' Yes, child, it 's a way he has.'

' Take off your bonnet, bebee ; perhaps he cannot see
your face.'

' I do not think that will be of much use, child ; how-
ever, I will take off my bonnet—there—and shake out my
hair—there—you have seen this hair before, sir, and this
face——'

' No answer, bebee.'

' Though the one was not quite so grey, nor the other so
wrinkled.'

'How came they so, bebee?'

'All along of this gorgio, child.'

'The gentleman in the house, you mean, bebee.'

'Yes, child, the gentleman in the house. God grant that I may preserve my temper. Do you know, sir, my name? My name is Herne, which signifies a hairy individual, though neither grey-haired nor wrinkled. It is not the nature of the Hernes to be grey or wrinkled, even when they are old, and I am not old.' . . .

'Time flows on, I engage in many matters, in most miscarry. Am sent to prison; says I to myself, I am become foolish. Am turned out of prison, and go back to the hairy ones, who receive me not over courteously; says I, for their unkindness, and my own foolishness, all the thanks to that gorgio. Answers to me the child, "I wish I could set eyes upon him, bebee."'

'I did so, bebee; go on.'

'"How shall I know him, bebee?" says the child. "Young and grey, tall, and speaks Romanly." Runs to me the child, and says, "I 've found him, bebee." "Where, child?" says I. "Come with me, bebee," says the child. "That 's he," says I, as I looked at my gentleman through the hedge.'

'Ha, ha! bebee, and here he lies, poisoned like a hog.'

'You have taken drows, sir,' said Mrs. Herne; 'do you hear, sir? drows; tip him a stave, child, of the song of poison.'

And thereupon the girl clapped her hands, and sang—

'The Rommany churl
And the Rommany girl,
To-morrow shall hie
To poison the sty,
And bewitch on the mead
The farmer's steed.'

'Do you hear that, sir?' said Mrs. Herne; 'the child has tipped you a stave of the song of poison: that is, she has sung it Christianly, though perhaps you would like to hear it Romanly; you were always fond of what was Roman. Tip it him Romanly, child.'

'He has heard it Romanly already, bebee; 'twas by that I found him out, as I told you.'

'Halloo, sir, are you sleeping? you have taken drows;
the gentleman makes no answer. God give me patience!'
'And what if he doesn't, bebee; isn't he poisoned like
a hog? Gentleman! indeed, why call him gentleman?
If he ever was one he's broke, and is now a tinker, a
worker of blue metal.'
'That's his way, child, to-day a tinker, to-morrow
something else; and as for being drabbed, I don't know
what to say about it.' . . .
'He is sick, child, sure enough. Ho, ho! sir, you have
taken drows; what, another throe! writhe, sir, writhe, the
hog died by the drow of gypsies; I saw him stretched
at evening. That's yourself, sir. There is no hope, sir,
no help, you have taken drow; shall I tell you your for-
tune, sir, your dukkerin? God bless you, pretty gentle-
man, much trouble will you have to suffer, and much water
to cross; but never mind, pretty gentleman, you shall be
fortunate at the end, and those who hate shall take off their
hats to you.'
'Hey, bebee!' cried the girl; 'what is this? what do
you mean? you have blessed the gorgio!'
'Blessed him! no, sure; what did I say? Oh, I
remember, I'm mad; well, I can't help it, I said what the
dukkerin dook told me; woe's me; he'll get up yet.'
'Nonsense, bebee! . . . He's drabbed, spite of dukkerin.'
'Don't say so, child; he's sick, 'tis true, but don't laugh
at dukkerin, only folks do that that know no better. I,
for one, will never laugh at the dukkerin dook. Sick
again; I wish he was gone.'
'He'll soon be gone, bebee; let's leave him. He's
as good as gone; look there, he's dead.'
'No, he's not, he'll get up—I feel it; can't we hasten
him?'
'Hasten him! yes, to be sure; set the dog upon him.
Here, juggal, look in there, my dog.'
The dog made its appearance at the door of the tent,
and began to bark and tear up the ground.
'At him, juggal, at him; he wished to poison, to drab
you. Halloo!'
The dog barked violently, and seemed about to spring
at my face, but retreated.

' The dog won't fly at him, child ; he flashed at the dog with his eye, and scared him. He 'll get up.'

' Nonsense, bebee ! you make me angry ; how should he get up ? '

' The dook tells me so, and, what 's more, I had a dream. I thought I was at York, standing amidst a crowd to see a man hung, and the crowd shouted, " There he comes ! " and I looked, and lo ! it was the tinker ; before I could cry with joy I was whisked away, and I found myself in Ely's big church, which was chock full of people to hear the dean preach, and all eyes were turned to the big pulpit ; and presently I heard them say, " There he mounts ! " and I looked up to the big pulpit, and lo ! the tinker was in the pulpit, and he raised his arm and began to preach. Anon, I found myself at York again, just as the drop fell, and I looked up, and I saw, not the tinker, but my own self hanging in the air.'

' You are going mad, bebee ; if you want to hasten him, take your stick and poke him in the eye.'

' That will be of no use, child, the dukkerin tells me so ; but I will try what I can do. Halloo, tinker ! you must introduce yourself into a quiet family, and raise confusion —must you ? You must steal its language, and, what was never done before, write it down Christianly—must you ? Take that—and that ' ; and she stabbed violently with her stick towards the end of the tent.

' That 's right, bebee, you struck his face ; now, once more, and let it be in the eye. Stay, what 's that ? get up, bebee.'

' What 's the matter, child ? '

' Some one is coming, come away.'

' Let me make sure of him, child ; he 'll be up yet.' And thereupon, Mrs. Herne, rising, leaned forward into the tent, and supporting herself against the pole, took aim in the direction of the farther end. ' I will thrust out his eye,' said she ; and, lunging with her stick, she would probably have accomplished her purpose had not at that moment the pole of the tent given way, whereupon she fell to the ground, the canvas falling upon her and her intended victim.

' Here 's a pretty affair, bebee,' screamed the girl.

'He 'll get up yet,' said Mrs. Herne, from beneath the canvas.

'Get up !—get up yourself ; where are you ? where is your—— Here, there, bebee, here 's the door; there, make haste, they are coming.'

'He 'll get up yet,' said Mrs. Herne, recovering her breath ; 'the dook tells me so.'

'Never mind him or the dook ; he is drabbed ; come away, or we shall be grabbed—both of us.'

'One more blow, I know where his head lies.'

'You are mad, bebee ; leave the fellow—gorgio avella.'

And thereupon the females hurried away.

George Borrow.

Poisoning the Porker

LISTEN to me ye Roman lads, who are seated in the straw about the fire, and I will tell how we poison the porker, I will tell how we poison the porker.

We go to the house of the poison-monger, where we buy three pennies' worth of bane, and when we return to our people, we say we will poison the porker ; we will try and poison the porker.

We then make up the poison, and then we take our way to the house of the farmer, as if to beg a bit of victuals, a little broken victuals.

We see a jolly porker, and then we say in Roman language, 'Fling the bane yonder amongst the dirt, and the porker soon will find it, the porker soon will find it.'

Early on the morrow, we will return to the farm-house, and beg the dead porker, the body of the dead porker.

And so we do, even so we do ; the porker dieth during the night; on the morrow we beg the porker, and carry to the tent the porker.

And then we wash the inside well, till all the inside is perfectly clean, till there 's no bane within it, not a poison grain within it.

And then we roast the body well, send for ale to the ale-house, and have a merry banquet, a merry Roman banquet.

The fellow with the fiddle plays, he plays ; the little lassie sings, she sings an ancient Roman ditty ; now hear the Roman ditty.

George Borrow.

Warlocks and Gypsies

WITCHES, warlocks and gypsies soon ken ae the ither.

Scots Proverb.

How to tell a Witch

A WITCH may be known by her hair, which is straight for three or four inches and then begins to curl—like a waterfall which comes down smoothly and then rebounds roundly on the neck.

Charles Godfrey Leland.

Othello and the Egyptian Spell

OTHELLO. I have a salt and sorry rheum offends me.
　　Lend me thy handkerchief.
DESDEMONA.　　　　　　　　Here, my lord.
OTHELLO. That which I gave you.
DESDEMONA.　　　　　　　I have it not about me.
OTHELLO. Not ?
DESDEMONA.　　　No, indeed, my lord.
OTHELLO. That's a fault. That handkerchief
　　Did an Egyptian to my mother give ;
　　She was a charmer, and could almost read
　　The thoughts of people ; she told her, while she kept it,
　　'Twould make her amiable, and subdue my father
　　Entirely to her love, but if she lost it
　　Or made a gift of it, my father's eye
　　Should hold her loathed, and his spirits should hunt
　　After new fancies. She dying gave it me ;
　　And bid me, when my fate would have me wive,
　　To give it her. I did so : and take heed on 't ;
　　Make it a darling like your precious eye ;
　　To lose 't or give 't away, were such perdition
　　As nothing else could match.

DESDEMONA.   Is 't possible ?
OTHELLO. "Tis true ; there 's magic in the web of it :
  A sibyl, that had number'd in the world
  The sun to course two hundred compasses,
  In her prophetic fury sew'd the work :
  The worms were hallow'd that did breed the silk ;
  And it was dyed in mummy which the skilful
  Conserved of maidens' hearts.

Shakespeare.

Magic

MAGIC did not jump at once into being, as to the thing itself ; it was not a revelation from hell, made at once to mankind, to tell them what they might do : the Devil did not come and offer his service gratis to us, and representing how useful a slave he would be, solicit us to take him into pay, and this at once, without ceremony or introduction. . . .

Not but that the Devil was very ready, when he found himself made necessary ; I say, he was very ready to come into the schemes when proposed, and to serve us in our occasion, and that with a willingness which was extremely obliging ; which showed him to be a person of abundance of complaisance, and mighty willing to engage us, whatever it cost him ; as much as to say, he was glad he could serve us, was ready to do his utmost for us, and the like.

Now to go back briefly to the occasion which brought the magicians to the necessity of seeking to him for assistance, and to take him into the management of their affairs ; the case was, in short, this : the world, as I have said already, began to be wiser than the ages before them : the ordinary magic of the former ages would not pass any longer for wisdom ; and if the wise men, as they were called, did not daily produce some new discoveries, it was evident the price and rate of soothsaying would come down to nothing. . . .

At first the magicians satisfied the curiosity of the people by juggle and trick, by framing artificial voices and noises ; foretelling strange events, by mechanical appearances, and

all the cheats which we find put upon the ignorant people
to this day ; and it would be tedious to enumerate the par-
ticulars by which they imposed upon one another. You
may guess at them by such as are mentioned before ; but
principally those who studied the heavenly motions, had
great opportunities of recommending themselves for men
of craft, pretending to tell fortunes, calculate nativities,
resolve doubts, read the lines of nature drawn in the face,
palms of the hand, symmetry of the body, moles and marks
on the flesh, and the like.

These things they carried to a due length, and we find
the success was so much to their advantage, that the whole
world, or great part of it, has been gipsey-ridden by them,
even to this day.

Daniel Defoe.

The Cousening Art of Sortilege
praĉtised especiallie by Aegyptian vagabonds

THE counterfeit *Aegyptians*, which were indeed cousen-
ing vagabonds, praĉtising the art called *Sortilegium*, had
no small credit among the multitude : howbeit, their
divinations were as was their fast and loose, and as the
witches cures and hurtes, & as the soothsaiers answers,
and as the conjurors raisings up of spirits, and as *Apollos*
or the Rood of graces oracles, and as the jugglers knacks
of legierdemaine, and as the papists exorcismes, and as the
witches charmes, and as the counterfeit visions, and as the
couseners knaveries. Hereupon it was said ; *Non inve-
niatur inter vos menahas*, that is *Sortilegus*, which were like
to these Aegyptian couseners.

Reginald Scot, 1584.

The People of Dar-Bushi-Fal

'NOT far from this place is a Char Seharra, or witch-
hamlet, where dwell those of the Dar-bushi-fal.
These are very evil people, and powerful enchanters ; for
it is well known that if any traveller stop to sleep in their
Char, they will with their sorceries, if he be a white man,
turn him as black as a coal, and will afterwards sell him as

a negro. Horses and mules they serve in the same manner, for if they are black, they will turn them red, or any other colour which best may please them ; and although the owners demand justice of the authorities, the sorcerers always come off best. They have a language which they use among themselves, very different from all other languages, so much so that it is impossible to understand them. They are very swarthy, quite as much so as mulattos, and their faces are exceedingly lean. As for their legs, they are like reeds ; and when they run, the devil himself cannot overtake them. They tell Dar-bushi-fal with flour ; they fill a plate, and then they are able to tell you anything you ask them. They likewise tell it with a shoe ; they put it in their mouth, and then they will recall to your memory every action of your life. They likewise tell Dar-bushi-fal with oil ; and indeed are, in every respect, most powerful sorcerers.

'Two women, once on a time, came to Fez, bringing with them an exceedingly white donkey, which they placed in the middle of the square called Faz el Bali ; they then killed it, and cut it into upwards of thirty pieces. Upon the ground there was much of the donkey's filth and dung ; some of this they took in their hands, when it straight assumed the appearance of fresh dates. . . . After they had collected much money from the spectators, one of them took a needle, and ran it into the tail of the donkey, crying " Arrhe li dar " (Get home), whereupon the donkey instantly rose up, and set off running, kicking every now and then most furiously ; and it was remarked, that not one single trace of blood remained upon the ground, just as if they had done nothing to it. Both these women were of the very same Char Seharra which I have already mentioned. They likewise took paper, and cut it into the shape of a peseta, and a dollar, and a half dollar, until they had made many pesetas and dollars, and then they put them into an earthen pan over a fire, and when they took them out, they appeared just fresh from the stamp, and with such money these people buy all they want.

'There was a friend of my grandfather, who came frequently to our house, who was in the habit of making this money. One day he took me with him to buy white silk ;

and when they had shown him some, he took the silk in his hand, and pressed it to his mouth, and then I saw that the silk, which was before white, had become green, even as grass. The master of the shop said, " Pay me for my silk." " Of what colour was your silk ? " he demanded. " White," said the man ; whereupon, turning round, he cried, " Good people, behold, the white silk is green " ; and so he got a pound of silk for nothing ; and he also was of the Char Seharra.

' They are very evil people indeed, and the Emperor himself is afraid of them. The poor wretch who falls into their hands has cause to rue ; they always go badly dressed, and exhibit every appearance of misery, though they are far from being miserable. Such is the life they lead.'

George Borrow.

The Gypsy Glamour

I REMEMBER to have heard (certainly very long ago, for at that time I believed the legend) that a gypsy exercised his glamour over a number of people at Haddington, to whom he exhibited a common dung-hill cock, trailing, what appeared to the spectators, a massy oaken trunk. An old man passed with a cart of clover ; he stopped and picked out a four-leaved blade ; the eyes of the spectators were opened, and the oaken trunk appeared to be a bulrush.

Sir Walter Scott.

Taw and the Wizard

' AND ever after that,' said Siani, ' the place was haunted.'

' Who haunted it ? '

' No one rightly knew that. It might have been the serving-man or it might have been the old lady herself, but any way it was a bad spirit, and the family had to leave the house, which fell all into ruins. But the old gate-keeper and his wife lived on at the little lodge, and often in the night they would be awakened by a bellowing like ten thousand bulls. Then they would see a light come through the gate ; it would stop there and laugh. After that the ruined house would be all lit up, and as the light died away the great laughter would come again.

'The people who lived about there were afraid to go near the house, and the fields where we Gypsies used to play, where we found hedgehogs and killed rabbits, were all deserted. At last they sent for a Wise Man to lay the ghost. He, and the minister, and the people all prayed together for four nights in succession, from midnight to one o'clock in the morning, but it was not until the fourth night, after the minister and the people had gone home, that the ghost was laid.' . . .

'What I tell you is true, every word. No one was there, only Taw and the Wise Man, and I to carry the things, for Taw liked me better nor any of her own daughters.' . . .

'The Wise Man took a bottle with water in it ; he lit a candle and put it in the bottle ; he read something from a book. Then he and the old Gypsy woman (I don't like to say her name, God rest her soul ! she was always good to me) knelt down hand in hand by the book and spoke the words together ; I could not hear what they said.' . . .

'The Wise Man blindfolded the old woman and led her across the field ; she carried the bottle and the bad devil that was in it. They went down the steps into the boat-house, and there the two knelt again. Then the old Gypsy gave the bottle to the Wise Man and spoke the words, while he dropped it into the lake. Now the ghost was laid, he was under the water, and troubled the place no more.' . . .

'They came back to the field where they had left me and the book. The Wise Man took a box from his pocket. " There, old woman, take this, open it ! " A toad jumped from the box ; there was a name written on its back. " Breathe into its mouth," he said, " and I will do so after thee." This was to bind her to him, so that he could call on her again. He paid her well for her help ; she bought many things with the money he gave her, new horses, new harps and fiddles for her sons, and new dresses for her daughters.'

M. Eileen Lyster.

A Blood Bond

A ND then one day the Thing happened. Archelaus, his wife, and sister-in-law had gone to attend a distant fair—the man to buy and sell horses, the women to tell fortunes. The girl and her grandmother were the only Romané left on the field. Piggott was sitting in the girl's tent pointing pinthorns with his knife, while he entertained her with a lively account of the gypsies of the Alhambra. Eldorai, a charming barbaric figure, with coral necklet and half-guinea pieces braided in her hair, crouched by the fire, her slim bare legs tucked under her. Lazily and happily he watched her kneading a little flour into dough, the simple constituent of the *Romani marikli* or gypsy cake. Suddenly the young girl said in a voice that thrilled him : ' Stephen '—it was the first time she had called him by his name—' I want some of your blood.' ' Splendidly dramatic,' thought Piggott, ' this is, no doubt, the prelude to a new version of the Robber Bridegroom, or, better still, perhaps to a vampire myth picked up five centuries ago, when her ancestors sojourned in the Balkans. However, a young and pretty vampire must be treated with the respect due to a lady.' Laughingly, he extended his arm, saying, ' Take it, little witch.' And then Eldorai, with her eyes fixed upon his, had rolled up his sleeve. And before he had time to realise what was happening, he felt himself stabbed in the fore-arm by some pointed instrument, doubtless one of the pinthorns of his own fashioning. The blood flowed. In a moment she had stanched it with the dough. He saw that it made a small scarlet blot on the paste. Then, though more deliberately, she had bared her shapely brown arm, and repeated this strange rite on her own person. Absorbed as an anthropologist observing for the first time some savage ceremony, Piggott watched her re-knead the dough in which their blood was now mingled, fashion it into a thin flat cake, and place it on the red ashes.

His collector's instincts aroused, he waited breathlessly for the next act in this mystery. In a few minutes the *marikli* was baked. Breaking it into two pieces, Eldorai

took one herself and handed the other to Piggott, gazing
intently into his eyes.

And Piggott, following her example, had eaten it. That
was the incredible part of it. How he, delicate-minded
and fastidious as he was, could ever have done so he was
afterwards at a loss to comprehend. He could only come
to the conclusion that he had been hypnotised by the girl,
just as spectators are by the Indian juggler in his famous
rope trick. But at the time he had felt neither discomfort
nor disgust; instead, a strange happiness had pervaded his
whole being. It was not until the next morning, when he
recalled the occurrence with a shudder, that he felt as
though he had taken part in the celebration of some sacri-
legious Black Mass.

Piggott remembered the words that Eldorai had spoken
to him with such extraordinary gravity: 'And now,
Stephen, you belongs to me and I belongs to you: and I
will come for you, my rom, to the day, no matter where-
soever I be, even if I has to wait until the seven years is
out.'   *Cornhill Magazine*, 1922.

The Sapengro

ONE day it happened that, being on my rambles, I
entered a green lane which I had never seen before;
at first it was rather narrow, but as I advanced it became
considerably wider; in the middle was a drift-way with
deep ruts, but right and left was a space carpeted with a
sward of trefoil and clover; there was no lack of trees,
chiefly ancient oaks, which, flinging out their arms from
either side, nearly formed a canopy, and afforded a pleasing
shelter from the rays of the sun, which was burning fiercely
above. Suddenly a group of objects attracted my atten-
tion. Beneath one of the largest of the trees, upon the
grass, was a kind of low tent or booth, from the top of
which a thin smoke was curling; beside it stood a couple
of light carts, whilst two or three lean horses or ponies
were cropping the herbage which was growing nigh.
Wondering to whom this odd tent could belong, I advanced
till I was close before it, when I found that it consisted of
two tilts, like those of waggons, placed upon the ground

and fronting each other, connected behind by a sail or large piece of canvas, which was but partially drawn across the top ; upon the ground in the intervening space was a fire, over which, supported by a kind of iron crow-bar, hung a cauldron. My advance had been so noiseless as not to alarm the inmates, who consisted of a man and woman, who sat apart, one on each side of the fire ; they were both busily employed—the man was carding plaited straw, whilst the woman seemed to be rubbing something with a white powder, some of which lay on a plate beside her. Suddenly the man looked up, and, perceiving me, uttered a strange kind of cry, and the next moment both the woman and himself were on their feet and rushing out upon me.

I retreated a few steps, yet without turning to flee. I was not, however, without apprehension, which, indeed, the appearance of these two people was well calculated to inspire. The woman was a stout figure, seemingly between thirty and forty ; she wore no cap, and her long hair fell on either side of her head, like horse-tails, half way down to her waist ; her skin was dark and swarthy, like that of a toad, and the expression of her countenance was particularly evil ; her arms were bare, and her bosom was but half-concealed by a slight bodice, below which she wore a coarse petticoat, her only other article of dress. The man was somewhat younger, but of a figure equally wild ; his frame was long and lathy, but his arms were remarkably short, his neck was rather bent, he squinted slightly, and his mouth was much awry ; his complexion was dark, but, unlike that of the woman, was more ruddy than livid ; there was a deep scar on his cheek, something like the impression of a halfpenny. The dress was quite in keeping with the figure : in his hat, which was slightly peaked, was stuck a peacock's feather ; over a waistcoat of hide, untanned and with the hair upon it, he wore a rough jerkin of russet hue ; smallclothes of leather, which had probably once belonged to a soldier, but with which pipeclay did not seem to have come in contact for many a year, protected his lower man as far as the knee ; his legs were cased in long stockings of blue worsted, and on his shoes he wore immense old-fashioned buckles.

Such were the two beings who now came rushing upon me ; the man was rather in advance, brandishing a ladle in his hand.

'So I have caught you at laſt,' said he ; 'I 'll teach ye, you young highwayman, to come skulking about my properties ! '

Young as I was, I remarked that his manner of speaking was different from that of any people with whom I had been in the habit of associating. It was quite as ſtrange as his appearance, and yet it nothing resembled the foreign English which I had been in the habit of hearing through the palisades of the prison ; he could scarcely be a foreigner.

'Your properties ! ' said I ; 'I am in the King's Lane. Why did you put them there, if you did not wish them to be seen ? '

'On the spy,' said the woman, 'hey ? I 'll drown him in the sludge in the toad-pond over the hedge.'

'So we will,' said the man, 'drown him anon in the mud.'

'Drown me, will you ? ' said I ; 'I should like to see you ! What 's all this about ? Was it because I saw you with your hands full of ſtraw-plait, and my mother there——'

'Yes,' said the woman ; 'what was I about ? '

MYSELF. 'How should I know ? Making bad money perhaps ! '

And it will be well here to observe that at this time there was much bad money in circulation in the neighbourhood, generally supposed to be fabricated by the prisoners. . . .

'I 'll ſtrangle thee,' said the beldame dashing at me. 'Bad money, is it ? '

'Leave him to me, wifelkin,' said the man interposing ; 'you shall now see how I 'll baſte him down the lane.'

MYSELF. 'I tell you what, my chap, you had better put down that thing of yours ; my father lies concealed within my tepid breaſt, and if to me you offer any harm or wrong, I 'll call him forth to help me with his forked tongue.'

MAN. 'What do you mean, ye Bengui's bantling ? I never heard such discourse in all my life ; playman's speech or Frenchman's talk—which, I wonder ? Your father !

tell the mumping villain that if he comes near my fire, I 'll serve him out as I will you. Take that—— Tiny Jesus! what have we got here? Oh, delicate Jesus! what is the matter with the child?'

I had made a motion which the viper understood; and now, partly disengaging itself from my bosom, where it had lain perdu, it raised its head to a level with my face, and stared upon my enemy with its glittering eyes.

The man stood like one transfixed, and the ladle with which he had aimed a blow at me now hung in the air like the hand which held it; his mouth was extended, and his cheeks became of a pale yellow, save alone that place which bore the mark which I have already described, and this shone now portentously, like fire. He stood in this manner for some time; at last the ladle fell from his hand, and its falling appeared to rouse him from his stupor.

'I say, wifelkin,' said he in a faltering tone, 'did you ever see the like of this here?'

But the woman had retreated to the tent, from the entrance of which her loathly face was now thrust, with an expression partly of terror and partly of curiosity. After gazing some time longer at the viper and myself, the man stooped down and took up the ladle; then, as if somewhat more assured, he moved to the tent, where he entered into conversation with the beldame in a low voice. Of their discourse, though I could hear the greater part of it, I understood not a single word; and I wondered what it could be, for I knew by the sound that it was not French. At last, the man, in a somewhat louder tone, appeared to put a question to the woman, who nodded her head affirmatively, and in a moment or two produced a small stool, which she delivered to him. He placed it on the ground, close by the door of the tent, first rubbing it with his sleeve, as if for the purpose of polishing its surface.

MAN. 'Now, my precious little gentleman, do sit down here by the poor people's tent; we wish to be civil in our slight way. Don't be angry and say no; but look kindly upon us and satisfied, my precious little God Almighty.'

WOMAN. 'Yes, my gorgious angel, sit down by the poor bodies' fire, and eat a sweetmeat. We want to ask you a question or two; only first put that serpent away.'

MYSELF. 'I can sit down and bid the serpent go to sleep, that's easy enough; but as for eating a sweetmeat, how can I do that? I have not got one, and where am I to get it?'

WOMAN. 'Never fear, my tiny tawny, we can give you one, such as you never ate, I dare say, however far you may have come from.'

The serpent sunk into its usual resting-place, and I sat down on the stool. The woman opened a box, and took out a strange little basket or hamper, not much larger than a man's fist, and formed of a delicate kind of matting. It was sewed at the top; but ripping it open with a knife she held it to me, and I saw, to my surprise, that it contained candied fruits of a dark green hue, tempting enough to one of my age. 'There, my tiny,' said she; 'taste and tell me how you like them.'

'Very much,' said I; 'where did you get them?'

The beldame leered upon me for a moment, then, nodding her head thrice with a knowing look, said: 'Who knows better than yourself, my tawny?'

Now, I knew nothing about the matter; but I saw that these strange people had conceived a very high opinion of the abilities of their visitor, which I was nothing loath to encourage. I therefore answered boldly: 'Ah, who indeed?'

'Certainly,' said the man; 'who should know better than yourself, or so well? And now, my tiny one, let me ask you one thing—you didn't come to do us any harm?'

'No,' said I, 'I had no dislike to you; though if you were to meddle with me——'

MAN. 'Of course, my gorgious, of course you would; and quite right too. Meddle with you!—what right have we? I should say it would not be quite safe. I see how it is; you are one of them there'; and he bent his head towards his left shoulder.

MYSELF. 'Yes, I am one of them—for I thought he was alluding to the soldiers,—you had best mind what you are about, I can tell you.'

MAN. 'Don't doubt we will for our own sake; Lord bless you, wifelkin, only think that we should see one of them there when we least thought about it. Well, I have heard of such things, though I never thought to see one ; however, seeing is believing. Well ! now you are come, and are not going to do us any mischief, I hope you will stay ; you can do us plenty of good if you will.'

MYSELF. ' What good can I do you ? '

MAN. ' What good ? plenty ! Would you not bring us luck ? I have heard say that one of them there always does, if it will but settle down. Stay with us, you shall have a tilted cart all to yourself if you like. We 'll make you our little God Almighty, and say our prayers to you every morning.'

MYSELF. ' That would be nice ; and if you were to give me plenty of these things, I should have no objection. But what would my father say ? I think he would hardly let me.'

MAN. ' Why not ? he would be with you, and kindly would we treat him. Indeed, without your father, you would be nothing at all.'

George Borrow.

Saul and the Witch of Endor

NOW Samuel was dead, and all Israel had lamented him, and buried him in Ramah, even in his own city. And Saul had put away those that had familiar spirits, and the wizards, out of the land. And the Philistines gathered themselves together, and came and pitched in Shunem : and Saul gathered all Israel together, and they pitched in Gilboa. And when Saul saw the host of the Philistines, he was afraid, and his heart greatly trembled. And when Saul inquired of the Lord, the Lord answered him not, neither by dreams, nor by Urim, nor by prophets. Then said Saul unto his servants, Seek me a woman that hath a familiar spirit, that I may go to her, and inquire of her. And his servants said to him, Behold, there is a woman that hath a familiar spirit at Endor. And Saul disguised himself, and put on other raiment, and he went, and two men with him, and they came to the woman by night : and he said, I pray thee, divine unto me by the familiar spirit, and bring me him up, whom I shall name unto thee. And the woman said unto him, Behold, thou knowest what

Saul hath done, how he hath cut off those that have familiar
spirits, and the wizards, out of the land : wherefore then
layest thou a snare for my life, to cause me to die ?   And
Saul sware to her by the Lord, saying, As the Lord liveth,
there shall no punishment happen to thee for this thing.
Then said the woman, Whom shall I bring up unto thee ?
And he said, Bring me up Samuel.   And when the woman
saw Samuel, she cried with a loud voice : and the woman
spake to Saul, saying, Why hast thou deceived me ? for
thou art Saul.   And the king said unto her, Be not afraid :
for what sawest thou ?   And the woman said unto Saul,
I saw gods ascending out of the earth.   And he said unto
her, What form is he of ?   And she said, An old man
cometh up ; and he is covered with a mantle.   And Saul
perceived that it was Samuel, and he stooped with his face
to the ground, and bowed himself.

And Samuel said to Saul, Why hast thou disquieted me,
to bring me up ?   And Saul answered, I am sore distressed ;
for the Philistines make war against me, and God is de-
parted from me, and answereth me no more, neither by
prophets, nor by dreams : therefore I have called thee,
that thou mayest make known unto me what I shall do.
Then said Samuel, Wherefore then dost thou ask of me,
seeing the Lord is departed from thee, and is become thine
enemy ?   And the Lord hath done to him, as he spake by
me : for the Lord hath rent the kingdom out of thine
hand, and given it to thy neighbour, even to David :
because thou obeyedst not the voice of the Lord, nor
executedst his fierce wrath upon Amalek, therefore hath
the Lord done this thing unto thee this day.   Moreover
the Lord will also deliver Israel with thee into the hand
of the Philistines : and to morrow shalt thou and thy sons
be with me : the Lord also shall deliver the host of Israel
into the hand of the Philistines.

Then Saul fell straightway all along on the earth, and was
sore afraid, because of the words of Samuel : and there
was no strength in him ; for he had eaten no bread all the
day, nor all the night.   And the woman came unto Saul,
and saw that he was sore troubled, and said unto him,
Behold, thine handmaid hath obeyed thy voice, and I have
put my life in my hand, and have hearkened unto thy words

which thou spakest unto me. Now therefore, I pray thee, hearken thou also unto the voice of thine handmaid, and let me set a morsel of bread before thee ; and eat, that thou mayest have strength, when thou goest on thy way. But he refused, and said, I will not eat.   1 *Samuel.*

The Tale of Aristomenus

IN speaking these words, and devising with my selfe of our departing the next morrow, lest Meroe the Witch should play by us as she had done by divers other persons, it fortuned that Socrates did fall asleepe, and slept very soundly, by reason of his travell, and plenty of meat and wine wherewithall hee had filled himselfe. Wherefore I closed and barred fast the doores of the chamber, and put my bed behinde the doore, and so layed mee downe to rest. But I could in no wise sleepe, for the great feare which was in my heart, untill it was about midnight, and then I began to slumber. But alas, behold suddenly the chamber doores brake open, and lockes, bolts, and posts fell downe, that you would verily have thought that some Theeves had beene presently come to have spoyled and robbed us. And my bed whereon I lay being a truckle bed, fashioned in forme of a Cradle, and one of the feet broken and rotten, by violence was turned upside downe, and I likewise was overwhelmed and covered lying in the same. Then perceived I in my selfe, that certaine affects of the minde by nature doth chance contrary. For as tears oftentimes trickle down the cheekes of him that seeth or heareth some joyfull newes, so I being in this fearefull perplexity, could not forbeare laughing, to see how of Aristomenus I was made like unto a snaile in his shell. And while I lay on the ground covered in this sort, I peeped under the bed to see what would happen. And behold there entred in two old women, the one bearing a burning torch, and the other a sponge and a naked sword : and so in this habit they stood about Socrates being fast asleep. Then shee which bare the sword sayd unto the other, Behold sister Panthia, this is my deare and sweet heart, which both day and night hath abused my wanton youthfulnesse. This is he, who little regarding my love, doth not onely defame me with

reproachfull words, but also intendeth to run away. And
I shall be forsaken by like craft as Vlysses did use, and shall
continually bewaile my solitarinesse as Calipso. Which
said, shee pointed towards mee that lay under the bed, and
shewed me to Panthia. This is hee, quoth she, which is
his Counsellor, and perswadeth him to forsake me, and
now being at the point of death he lieth proſtrate on the
ground covered with his bed, and hath seene all our doings,
and hopeth to escape scot-free from my hands, but I will
cause that hee shall repent himselfe too late, nay rather
forthwith, of his former untemperate language, and his
present curiosity. Which words when I heard I fell into
a cold sweat, and my heart trembled with feare, insomuch
that the bed over me did likewise rattle and shake. Then
spake Panthia unto Meroe and said, Siſter let us by and by
teare him in pieces, or tye him by the members, and so cut
them off. Then Meroe (being so named because she was
a Taverner, and loved wel good wines) answered, Nay
rather let him live, and bury the corps of this poore wretch
in some hole of the earth ; and therewithall shee turned
the head of Socrates on the other side, and thruſt her sword
up to the hilts into the left part of his necke, and received
the bloud that gushed out, into a pot, that no drop thereof
fell beside : which things I saw with myne owne eyes,
and as I thinke to the intent she might alter nothing that
pertained to sacrifice, which she accuſtomed to make,
she thruſt her hand downe into the intrals of his body, and
searching about, at length brought forth the heart of my
miserable companion Socrates, who having his throat cut
in such sort, yeelded out a dolefull cry and gave up the
ghoſt. Then Panthia ſtopped the wide wound of his
throat with the Sponge, and said, O Sponge sprung and
made of the sea, beware that thou passe not by running
River. This being sayd, the one of them moved and turned
up my bed, and then they ſtrid over mee and went their
wayes, and the doores closed faſt, the poſts ſtood in their
old places, and the lockes and bolts were shut againe. But
I that lay upon the ground like one without soule, naked
and cold, like to one that were more than halfe dead, yet
reviving my selfe, and appointed as I thought for the
Gallowes, began to say, Alasse what shall become of me

to morrow, when my companion shall be found murthered here in the chamber ? To whom shall I seeme to tell any similitude of truth, when as I shall tell the trueth in deed ? They will say, If thou wert unable to resist the violence of the women, yet shouldest thou have cried for helpe ; Wouldst thou suffer the man to be slaine before thy face and say nothing ? Or why did they not slay thee likewise ? Why did they spare thee that stood by and saw them commit that horrible fact ? Wherefore although thou hast escaped their hands, yet thou shalt not escape ours. While I pondered these things with my selfe the night passed on, and so I resolved to take my horse before day, and goe forward on my journy.

Howbeit the wayes were unknowne unto me, and thereupon I tooke up my packet, unlocked and unberred the doors, but those good and faithfull doores which in the night did open of their owne accord, could then scantly be opened with their keyes. And when I was out I cried, O sirrah Hostler where art thou ? open the stable doore, for I will ride away by and by. The Hostler lying behinde the stable doore upon a pallet, and halfe asleepe, What (quoth hee) doe you not know that the wayes be very dangerous ? What meane you to rise at this time of night ? If you perhaps guilty of some heynous crime, be weary of your life, yet thinke you not that wee are such Sots that we will die for you. Then said I, It is well nigh day, and moreover, what can Theeves take from him that hath nothing ? Doest thou not know (Foole as thou art) if thou be naked, if ten Gyants should assaile thee, they could not spoyle or rob thee ? Whereunto the drowsie Hostler halfe asleepe, and turning on the other side, answered, What know I whether you have murthered your Companion whom you brought in yesternight, or no, and now seeke the meanes to escape away ? O Lord, at that time I remember the earth seemed to open, and me thought I saw at hell gate the Dog Cerberus ready to devour mee ; and then I verily beleeved, that Meroe did not spare my throat, mooved with pitty, but rather cruelly pardoned mee to bring mee to the Gallowes. Wherefore I returned to my chamber, and there devised with my selfe in what sort I should finish my life. But when I saw that fortune would minister unto mee no other instrument, than that which my bed profered mee, I sayd, O bed, O bed, most dear unto me at this present, which hast abode and suffered with me so many miseries, judge and arbiter of such things as were done here this night, whome onely I may call to witnesse for my innocency, render (I say) unto me some wholsome weapon to end my life, that am most willing to dye. And therewithal I pulled out a piece of the rope wherewith the bed was corded, and tyed one end thereof about a rafter by the window, and with the other end I made a sliding knot, and stood upon my bed, and so put my neck into it, and when I leaped from the bed, thinking verily to strangle my selfe and so dye, behold the rope beeing old and rotten burst in the middle, and I fell downe tumbling upon Socrates that lay under : And even at that same very time the Hostler came in crying with a loud voyce, and sayd, Where are you that made such hast at midnight, and now lies wallowing abed ? Whereupon (I know not whether it was by my fall, or by the great cry of the Hostler) Socrates as waking out of a sleepe, did rise up first and sayd, It is not without cause that strangers do speake evill of all such Hostlers, for this Caitife in his comming in, and with his crying out, I thinke under a colour to steale away somthing, hath waked me out of a sound sleepe. Then I rose up joyfull with a merry coun-tenance, saying, Behold good Hostler, my friend, my com-panion and my brother, whom thou didst falsly affirme to be slaine by mee this night. And therewithall I embraced my friend Socrates and kissed him, and tooke him by the hand and sayd, Why tarry we ? Why lose wee the pleasure of this faire morning ? Let us goe, and so I tooke up my packet, and payed the charges of the house and departed : and we had not gone a mile out of the Towne but it was broad day, and then I diligently looked upon Socrates throat, to see if I could espy the place where Meroe thrust in her sword : but when I could not perceive any such thing, I thought with my selfe, What a mad man am I, that being overcome with wine yester night, have dreamed such terrible things ? Behold, I see Socrates is sound, safe, and in health. Where is his wound ? where is the Sponge ? Where is his great and new cut ? And then I spake to him

and sayd, Verily it is not without occasion, that Physitians
of experience do affirme, That such as fill their gorges
abundantly with meat and drinke, shall dreame of dire and
horrible sights: for I my selfe, not tempering my appetite
yeſter night from the pots of wine, did seeme to see this
night ſtrange and cruel visions, that even yet I think my
self sprinkled and wet with human blood : whereunto
Socrates made answer and said, Verily I my self dreamed
this night that my throat was cut, and that I felt the paine
of the wound, and that my heart was pulled out of my
belly, and the remembrance thereof makes me now to
feare, for my knees do so tremble that I can scarse goe any
further, and therefore I would faine eat somewhat to
strengthen and revive my spirits. Then said I, Behold
here thy breakefaſt, and therwithall I opened my scrip that
hanged upon my shoulder, and gave him bread and cheese,
and we sate downe under a great Plane tree, and I eat part
with him ; and while I beheld him eating greedily, I per-
ceived that he waxed meigre and pale, and that his lively
colour faded away, insomuch that beeing in great fear,
and remembring those terrible furies of whom I lately
dreamed, the firſt morsell of bread that I put in my mouth
(which was but very small) did so ſticke in my jawes, that
I could neither swallow it downe, nor yet yeeld it up, and
moreover the small time of our being together increased
my feare, and what is hee that seeing his companion die
in the highway before his face, would not greatly lament
and bee sorry ? But when that Socrates had eaten suffi-
ciently hee waxed very thirſty, for indeed he had well nigh
devoured all a whole Cheese : and behold evill fortune !
there was behinde the Plane tree a pleasant running water
as cleere as Cryſtal, and I sayd unto him, Come hither
Socrates to this water and drinke thy fill. And then he
rose and came to the River, and kneeled downe upon the
side of the banke to drinke, but he had scarce touched the
water with his lips, when as behold the wound of his throat
opened wide, and the Sponge suddenly fell into the water,
and after issued out a little remnant of bloud, and his body
being then without life, had fallen into the river, had not
I caught him by the leg and so pulled him up. And after
that I had lamented a good space the death of my wretched

companion, I buried him in the Sands there by the river.

Which done, in great feare I rode through many Outwayes and desart places, and as culpable of the death of Socrates, I forsooke my countrey, my wife, and my children, and came to Etolia where I married another Wife.

Apuleius.

The Red King and the Witch

IT was the Red King, and he bought ten ducats' worth of victuals. He cooked them, and put them in a press. And he locked the press, and from night to night posted people to guard the victuals.

In the morning, when he looked, he found the platters bare. He did not find anything in them. Then the king said : ' I will give the half of my kingdom to whoever shall be found to guard the press, that the victuals may not go amissing from it.'

The king had three sons. Then the eldest thought within himself. ' God ! what, give half the kingdom to a stranger ! It were better for me to watch. Be it unto me according to God's will.'

He went to his father : ' Father, all hail. What, give the kingdom to a stranger ! It were better for me to watch.'

And his father said to him : ' As God will, only don't be frightened by what you may see.'

Then he said : ' Be it unto me according to God's will.' And he went and lay down in the palace. And he put his head on the pillow, and remained with his head on the pillow till towards dawn. And a warm sleepy breeze came and lulled him to slumber. And his little sister arose. And she turned a somersault, and her nails became like an axe, and her teeth like a shovel. And she opened the cupboard, and ate up everything. Then she became a child again, and returned to her place in the cradle, for she was a child at the breast. The lad arose, and told his father that he had seen nothing. His father looked in the press, found the platters bare—no victuals, no anything. His father said to him : ' It would take a better man than you, and even he might do nothing.'

His middle son also said : ' Father, all hail ! I am going to watch to-night.'

' Go, dear ; only play the man.'

' Be it unto me according to God's will.'

And he went into the palace, and put his head on a pillow. And at ten o'clock came a warm breeze, and sleep seized him. Up rose his sister, and unwound herself from her swaddling-bands, and turned a somersault, and her teeth became like a shovel, and her nails like an axe. And she went to the press, and opened it, and ate off the platters what she found. She ate it all, and turned a somersault again, and went back to her place in the cradle. Day broke, and the lad arose, and his father asked him and said : ' It would take a better man than you, and yet he might not do anything for me, if he were as poor a creature as you.'

The youngest son arose. ' Father, all hail ! Give me also leave to watch the cupboard by night.'

' Go, dear ; only don't be frightened with what you see.'

' Be it unto me according to God's will,' said the lad.

And he went and took four needles, and lay down with his head on the pillow ; and he stuck the four needles in four places. When sleep seized him, he knocked his head against a needle, so he stayed awake till dawn. And his sister arose from her cradle, and he saw. And she turned a somersault, and he was watching her. And her teeth became like a shovel, and her nails like an axe. And she went to the press, and ate up everything. She left the platters bare. And she turned a somersault, and became tiny again as she was ; she went to her cradle. The lad, when he saw that, trembled with fear ; it seemed to him ten years till daybreak.

And he arose, and went to his father. ' Father, all hail ! '

Then his father asked him : ' Didst see anything, Peterkin ? '

' What did I see ? What did I not see ? Give me money and a horse, a horse fit to carry the money, for I am away to marry me.'

His father gave him ducats in abundance, and he put

them on his horse. The lad went, and made a hole on the border of the city. He made a chest of stone, and placed all the money there, and buried it. He placed a stone cross above, and departed. And he journeyed eight years, and came to the queen of all the birds that fly.

And the queen of the birds asked him : ' Whither away, Peterkin ? '

' Thither where there is neither death nor old age, to marry me.'

The queen said to him : ' Here is neither death nor old age.'

Then Peterkin said to her : ' How comes it that here is neither death nor old age ? '

Then she said to him : ' When I whittle away the wood of all this forest, then death will come and take me, and old age.'

Then Peterkin said : ' One day and one morning death will come and old age, and take me.'

And he departed farther, and journeyed on eight years, and arrived at a palace of copper. And a maiden came forth from that palace, and took him and kissed him. She said : ' I have waited long for thee.'   ·

She took the horse and put him in the stable, and he spent the night there. He arose in the morning, and placed his saddle on the horse.

Then the maiden began to weep, and asked him. ' Whither away, Peterkin ? '

' Thither, where there is neither death nor old age.'

Then the maiden said to him : ' Here is neither death nor old age.'

Then he asked her : ' How comes it that here is neither death nor old age ? '

' Why, when these mountains are levelled and these forests, then death will come.'

' This is no place for me,' said the lad to her. And he departed farther.

Then what said the horse to him ? ' Master, whip me four times, and twice yourself, for you are come to the Plain of Regret. And Regret will seize you, and cast you down, horse and all. So spur your horse, and escape and tarry not.'

He came to a hut. In the hut he beholds a lad, as it were ten years old, who asked him : ' What seekest thou, Peterkin, here ? '

' I seek the place where there is neither death nor old age.' The lad said : ' Here is neither death nor old age. I am the Wind.'

Then Peterkin said : ' Never, never will I go from here.' And he dwelt there a hundred years, and grew no older.

There the lad dwelt, and went out to hunt in the Mountains of Gold and Silver, and he could hardly carry home the game.

Then what said the Wind to him ? ' Peterkin, go unto all the Mountains of Gold and the Mountains of Silver ; but go not to the Mountain of Regret or to the Valley of Grief.'

He heeded not, but went to the Mountain of Regret and the Valley of Grief. And Grief cast him down ; he wept till his eyes were full.

And he went to the Wind : ' I am going home to my father, I will not stay longer.'

' Go not, for your father is dead, and brothers you have no more left at home. A million years have come and gone since then. The spot is not known where your father's palace stood. They have planted melons on it ; it is but an hour since I passed that way.'

But the lad departed thence, and arrived at the maiden's, whose was the palace of copper. Only one stick remained, and she cut it and grew old. As he knocked at the door, the stick fell, and she died. He buried her, and departed thence. And he came to the queen of the birds in the great forest. Only one branch remained, and that was all but through. When she saw him, she said, ' Peterkin, thou art quite young.'

Then he said to her, ' Dost thou remember telling me to stay here ? ' As she pressed and broke through the branch, she too fell and died.

He came where his father's palace stood and looked about him. There was no palace, no anything. And he fell to marvelling : ' God, Thou art mighty.' He only recognised his father's well, and went to the well. His sister, the witch, when she saw him, said to him : ' I have waited long for you, dog.' She rushed at him to devour him, but he made the sign of the cross, and she perished.

And he departed thence and came on an old man with his beard down to his belt. ' Father, where is the palace of the Red King ? I am his son.'

' What is this,' said the old man, ' thou tellest me, that thou art his son ? My father's father has told me of the Red King. His very city is no more. Dost thou not see it is vanished ? And dost thou tell me that thou art the Red King's son ? '

' It is not twenty years, old man, since I departed from my father, and dost thou tell me that thou knowest not my father ? ' (It was a million years since he had left his home.) ' Follow me, if thou dost not believe me.'

And he went to the cross of stone ; only a palm's breadth was out of the ground. And it took him two days to get at the chest of money. When he had lifted out the chest, and opened it, Death sat in one corner groaning, and Old Age groaning in another corner.

Then what said Old Age ? ' Lay hold of him, Death.'

' Lay hold of him, yourself.'

Old Age laid hold of him in front, and Death laid hold of him behind.

The old man took and buried him decently, and planted the cross near him. And the old man took the money and also the horse.

Rumanian Gypsy Folk-Tale.

Benison

FEAR no more the heat o' the sun,
      Nor the furious winter's rages ;
Thou thy worldly task hast done,
      Home art gone and ta'en thy wages :
Golden lads and girls all must,
As chimney-sweepers, come to dust.

BLACK ARTS

Fear no more the frown o' the great ;
   Thou art past the tyrant's stroke ;
Care no more to clothe and eat ;
   To thee the reed is as the oak :
The sceptre, learning, physic, must
All follow this and come to dust.

Fear no more the lightning-flash,
   Nor the all-dreaded thunder-stone ;
Fear not slander, censure rash ;
   Thou hast finish'd joy and moan :
All lovers young, all lovers must
Consign to thee and come to dust.

No exorciser harm thee !
Nor no witchcraft charm thee !
Ghost unlaid forbear thee !
Nothing ill come near thee !
Quiet consummation have ;
And renowned be thy grave !

Made in the USA
San Bernardino, CA
03 March 2020